mom vs debt

How I paid off $64k in credit card debt in under 3 years without becoming a stripper

Amanda Arthur Krill

All rights reserved. No part of this book may be reproduced, stored in a retrieval system, or transmitted in any form or by any means—electronic, mechanical, digital, photocopy, recording, or any other—except for brief quotations in printed reviews, without the prior permission of the author.

Published 2019 YGTMama Media Co. on YGTMama Inc. Trade Paperback Edition

The publisher is not responsible for websites (or their content) that are not owned by the publisher. Published in Canada, for Global Distribution by YGTMama Media Co. Press, a division of YGTMama Inc.

Copyright © 2019 by Amanda Arthur Krill

Mom Vs Debt

ISBN 978-1-9990188-3-2

Reviews

Amanda's writing is like candy for the soul. It's approachable and accessible with a side of no-bull-shit-wit and the tough love of a friend. I devoured this book in less than an hour and immediately got to work with some of her helpful resources for managing debt. I would recommend this book to anyone, mama or not, in debt or not.

~ Sabrina Greer, 4x best selling author, CEO YGTMama Inc, podcast host and clarity coach for moms.

I read this in under two hours, and I'm shocked. It's short, but eloquent; gets the point across and entertains all at once. Not the typical financial how-to at all, yet it gives the reader all the necessary tools to do it for themselves.

- Luisa Rey

This book is the next best thing to being able to sit down with Amanda at her kitchen table to ask how on earth she managed to pay off all that debt in only three years.

Despite being a subject most of us would rather avoid, it's an easy, fun read, that will have you feeling as though you're chatting over coffee with an old friend. Honest, warm, and funny, this little gem manages to both instruct and inspire.

- Lisa Wilder Kruk

I really appreciated how honest Amanda was about her experience, both of getting into debt and getting out of it again. It's like she's taking you by the hand and gently leading you on a journey, one without judgement (because who needs any more guilt around money than the stuff we already heap on ourselves?!?) but with grace and understanding.

I read this in one sitting (yes, I did the questions in my head!) but it's something I'll be going back to for a second read so I can absorb all the goodness more fully - and do the questions on a piece of paper this time. If you've ever struggled with conversations around money, I'd highly recommend this book. You don't have to wait until you're thousands of pounds in debt to benefit from it. Instead, read it today and maybe save yourself some of the heartache and worry

- El Edwards, Author

I absolutely love the way the author turned her mess into a message. Seeing her monetary screw ups and money mismanagement as an opportunity to get uncomfortable, lean into her faith, get uncomfortable and GROW was so inspiring and motivating to look at my own debt and spending habits and albeit "void filling".

I related so much to what the author shared with her readers! After reading Mom vs. Debt I feel compelled to dig deeper into my own spending habits, look my debt square in the face, follow her simple directions and get my debt under control! Heck if she can conquer 65 grand of debt, my 10 is a walk in the park!

- Jillian West

Contents

Introduction	9
ONE Debt Isn't the End of the World	11
TWO Back to the Beginning	14
THREE Money Is Not Evil	26
FOUR Money Mindset	32
FIVE Identify Your Why	40
SIX Budget Is Not A Bad Word	46
SEVEN Step By Step: How I Paid It Off	52
EIGHT There are No Mistakes	62
NINE Bonus Shiz	66

Dedication

To all the moms who've forgotten who they are.

Your kids need the real you, and I'm dedicated to help you get back to them as the real you.

Introduction

It should be said right from the start that I am not a financial guru. I do not have a degree in finance. I'm not even that good at taking care of my money yet.

But I'm getting there, and I know that my story will help a ton of people deal with any shame they feel around their debt.

My hope is that we can all collectively learn from the journey that I've been on, and that we can all do better.

But please understand that this is not a book about money. This is a book about looking at your own journey and realizing that there are no mistakes, only lessons to learn and new paths to take.

ONE

Debt is Not the End of the World

Do you know what isn't the worst thing in the world?

Being in debt.

It happens to just about everyone, after all. Unless you were born with a trust fund, or millionaire parents, at some point, you are going to spend more money than you make, and you are going to incur debt. (And sometimes, even if you DO have the trust fund and loaded parents, you will rack up some debt anyway.)

Humans are (mostly) not born being naturally great with money.

You know what we are great at, however? Wanting stuff. Buying stuff we can't afford. Disregarding our debt to income ratio.

So, chances are you bought this book because the title, *Mom Vs. Debt*, made you think to yourself, "Hey...that's me."

It's me too. At several points in my life, I've been in debt. I've dug holes bigger than I am tall. I've created mountains for myself that I was only able to scale with the assistance of a divine being (God...if that wasn't clear.) And I generally mucked up my life.

But all of those "mistakes" immediately preceded some of my greatest feats, so rather than dwelling on the mucking up, I choose to look at my less than stellar moments as a natural catalyst that propelled me, kicking and screaming, into my next phase.

I can say, with complete honesty, that every time I've found myself in debt, it's been because I was ignoring the nudges I felt to do something bigger and bolder with my life. I knew God was pushing me to change and surrender control to Him, but I was fighting Him with every ounce of my being.

Generally speaking, I wasted money and time just trying to keep my daily life stable, normal, and unchanged. I was actually tired of my life the way it was, but I wasn't willing to get out of my comfort zone. So instead, I spent money I didn't have on stuff I didn't need to fill up a hole I didn't realize needed filling.

So why am I so very vocal about my story? It's simply:

I want everyone to understand that debt is a thing that happens, but it's surely not the end of the world.

You may or may not have heard my story, so I'll just start at the beginning. (Feel free to skip this part if you've heard it already.)

TWO

Back to the Beginning

I got married young. Not like 16-years-old young, but I was still in the midst of college and not quite twenty-one yet when I said "I do."

My husband is a great guy who just happens to be really good with money. I am a woman who would rather stick my head in the sand and pretend like I've got loads of cash, than to actually sit down and add it all up.

We were both still in college when we got married; living in a tiny one-bedroom apartment in Maumee, Ohio, working at a hotel, and taking classes at The University of Toledo.

Rent was exactly $385 a month and tuition was just over $700. Not qualifying for financial aid, and not interested in student loans, we opted to scrape by. We only ate out once a month. We bought the bare minimum for groceries. We never turned our heat on (partially because of the smoker who lived next door and who we shared a vent with, and partially because our basement apartment sustained a temp of around 62 degrees year-round).

As you can imagine, life wasn't exactly the lap of luxury.

The intentional bonus of living like this was graduating from college with ZERO debt. I think my husband had a small loan before we got married, and he'd borrowed money from his grandmother, but basically, we owed nothing.

But, for me, living this way was harder than I let on. I didn't like being told I couldn't have something I wanted.

Well, that's the thing right there, isn't it? It wasn't that I was denying myself, rather it was that someone else denying me what I wanted.

It was, of course, in our best interest. This denial was to ensure that we would have a brighter future together, but from my limited perspective, it felt like I was being controlled.

It's worth mentioning here that a large percentage of my genealogical background is Scots-Irish. I didn't know it at the time, (Ancestry.com wasn't a thing yet), but the blood of the Scots runs strong in this one.

I've never felt anything more true than Mel Gibson

as William Wallace screaming, "They can take our lives, but they'll never take our FREEDOM."

Freedom is the one thing that matters to me more than anything. I'd rather live a destitute life, free to do what I like, than live in a golden cage atop a pile of money.

And I actually felt that those were my only options.

Fast-forward several years: I'm a twenty-eight-year-old mom with two kids who'd been born eighteen months apart. My husband was an English teacher. I stayed home with the little ones, and I was pregnant for the last time.

Being a mom is, by far, my greatest achievement. Raising three little people to be good humans is clearly the most important work of my life. It can, though, leave a woman feeling like an empty vessel. Or at least that's what happened to me.

I was pouring myself entirely into my kids and never replenishing my own wants and desires. I didn't even read anymore; an activity I once did voraciously. I was a shell of who I once was; all dreams and ideas had been abandoned for three tiny people who needed me.

I found myself selling things on eBay. First, things I found at garage sales. Old, rare things, like a Jem and the Holograms videotape, or my husband's

Transformers. Eventually, I started scouting for things that were regional, and would sell in other parts of the country.

There was a thrill to this sort of chase. I once sold a Toy Story Bullseye doll for $99 when I'd only I paid $9.99 for it initially.

We once drove six hours to buy a van load of John Deere comforters, because we could buy them for $39.99 and sell them for $250 a piece.

Eventually, that too, became overwhelming. Things stopped selling as well as they once did. I was bored. It was hard to get everything to the post office with three little kids afoot.

Then I heard about mystery shopping.

Yes, it's a real thing. A very real thing at that.

There are companies that will hire you to go through a McDonald's or Arby's drive-thru, order food, and then simply report back about the purchase experience. Staples did this, too. I even got a mystery shopping gig in Chicago that paid me $120 and reimbursed me for two meals. It was SUPER fun.

The real problem was that I had to sometimes drive two hours to report on a handful of "shops".

A shop consisted of visiting the establishment assigned (like a bank, a restaurant, or a retail store), making a purchase, interacting with at least one person, and then reporting back via an online report on what occurred.

I tried to schedule as many shops as I could for one day, usually toting all three kids along with me. I took notes. I filled out thorough reports. And, here's where it became sticky, I had a wicked bad habit of spending more than my given "allowance" for each shop.

For example, I would be allotted $2 to spend at Staples, and then actually spend $85. (What? I like office supplies…)

Having an income of my own emboldened me. I didn't "need" to ask my husband for money, because I had a little of my own.

I bought things for myself. I bought things for my kids. This ability, this freedom, to spend made me feel great.

I spent. I spent. And I overspent.

Eventually, the amount of money coming in for my mystery shopping was no match for what I was spending. I tried to supplement my income with substitute teaching, but the cost of childcare for three young children was astronomical.

I knew I was in trouble, but I had no idea how much debt I had actually incurred.

To be honest, I was just plain scared to add it all up.

It became increasingly clear that mystery shopping was only making my problems worse, but if I stopped doing that altogether, I had no income at all.

This is when I got creative.

It was 2006 and the Internet was just beginning to become what we know it as today. I found a few gigs writing for websites, mostly reviewing television shows, for a small fee. It brought in a little extra money and gave me the confidence I needed to look for even more opportunities.

This led me to look for actual, legitimate ways to make money from home. Today, this is a whole lot easier than it was back then. Just 10 short years ago, my options were mostly "taking surveys", multi-level marketing, or some other less than desirable option.

I carefully vetted each opportunity. Researching like I was getting paid for it, I eventually I found an idea that resonated.

Before kids, I worked briefly at a local television station as a producer for two shows, and as an administrative assistant to the station's director.

If I could do perform those duties in person, surely, I could do the same virtually, right?

Shortly after this epiphany, I started marketing

myself as a virtual assistant, and came across an ad on Craigslist (this was before people were being murdered for answering Craigslist ads…).

The guy who posted it gave me my first real shot as a virtual assistant.

I won't tell his story, as it's not mine to tell, but the gist is that he was working on a website to help couples stay together.

The idea was to give husbands and wives the tools to work through their problems. I worked tirelessly with him to schedule appointments with big insurance companies with the idea that happy people are healthy people.

And I did it. I actually got companies like Aetna, Humana and Blue Cross to meet with us.

The problem though? I was only making $8/hr for the entire two years he used my services.

Oh, but somehow, I haven't even told you about the debt yet.

Even when I first started working on the aforementioned project, I still wasn't quite sure what my cumulative debt was at that point. It was spread across several credit cards; including a joint one that my husband thought we had paid off.

I was making minimum payments on all the cards

and was at the point that I had them all maxed out. It became high time to really add it all up and see where I was, so I could make a plan to get rid of it.

Logic says you do this from the beginning. You keep track. You know what's going on.

I'm not always the most logical person, though.

So, when I sat down and added up all the balances, it rounded out to roughly $64,000.

Yes, you read that right.

Honestly, I have no idea what I spent all that money on. We didn't have a Lexus sitting in the garage. Nor had we been on a bunch of expensive trips. Mostly I spent it on stupid crap that I probably didn't even have anymore, on groceries, and on paying bills that I didn't really have the money to pay.

For most people, when staring down a barrel like that, it's easy for depression to take over. For me, though, it just lit a fire. It gave me purpose I had been lacking, and it caused me to get creative.

This harkens back to something I touched on earlier in this book. I'm sure that God was pushing me into a new direction, but I was hanging on for dear life right where I was.

My nature is generally one that does not resist change, but every once in a while, I dig my feet in where I'm standing like you wouldn't believe.

That's become a bit of a road sign for me. When I start down the path of spending rather frivolously, it's time to look at what I'm resisting in my life.

What am I procrastinating on?

Where do I need to change directions?

Once I recognize what's going on, I can reign spending in before things get out of hand again.

In the following chapters, I want to talk about money, why it's not actually the root of all evil, why you may have issues with it, and how we can change up the way we think about it to make it work for us (rather than against us).

I'm going to finish up with the exact way I got rid of all my debt. Feel free to use my method or develop one that works for you.

Are you like I was and don't have any idea how much debt you are actually in?

Use the following table to list out each account with how much you owe + the interest rate, too.

Actual Debt Analysis

BILL	STARTING BALANCE	INTEREST RATE	MINIMUM PAYMENT	DATE PAID OFF
			$	
			$	
			$	
			$	
			$	
			$	
			$	
			$	
			$	
			$	
			$	
			$	
			$	
			$	
			$	
			$	
			$	
			$	
			$	
			$	
			$	
			$	
			$	
			$	
			$	
			$	
			$	
			$	

TOTAL BILLS AMOUNT $

THREE

Money is not evil.

*I*f your childhood was anything like mine, I'm sure you've heard the phrase, "Money is the root of all evil," more than once.

I mean, you probably heard it a lot. Right up there with, "There's always something else that uses up all the extra money."

These are both erroneous and completely unhelpful statements. They lead to detrimental thought patterns that don't at all help you learn how to properly handle your money.

Let's look at the first one.

"Money is the root of all evil."

This is a hugely misquoted Bible verse. What it really says is, "The LOVE of money is the root of all evil."

That one word "love" is the real difference maker.

Loving money and having money are different. The

difference is this:

When you love something or someone in a way that it supplants everything else in your life – that's idolatry.

If you aren't familiar with the Ten Commandments, idolatry is number two on the list.

Money itself is not the problem. It's loving money to the point that it becomes more important than God, or your kids, or your wife that is the problem.

Having money isn't the issue. If none of us had any money, we wouldn't be able to tithe, and if you've read your bible, or ever been to a church service in your life, you know that the tithe is a pretty big deal.

A tithe is 10% of your income given to your local place of worship to help them keep the doors open.

If you aren't tithing, that's between you and God, but I'll tell you that when I do, I find that my income increases.

It's almost like God promised that if you give faithfully, you will get back even more.

Oh wait, that IS what He said.

Now, back to the discussion on loving money.

Having loads of it isn't loving it. Money is a transactional item that our society uses to trade goods and services.

There was a time in history that money did not exist and people still traded goods and services. Some people had more than others, even though money didn't exist. They were the "rich" people of their time, but they didn't have any money to love.

Understanding that difference is key to changing thought patterns about money.

Money is NOT evil;rather it's loving money that is. There is nothing wrong with having money. It doesn't make you a bad person. It also doesn't make you better than anyone else.

If you happen to have it, don't hoard it as that leads to loving it.

View the extra money you have as a way to do good in the world and help people when you can.

View the extra money you have as a way to do good in the world and help people when you can.

The second detrimental thought associated with money is that there is always going to be something that comes up every time you have a little extra.

This does happen, but it doesn't always happen.

If you are budgeting and managing your money well, you will have it when the unexpected comes up, and they won't hurt quite so badly.

This idea, much like money being evil, is impervious. It digs itself into our collective psyche in a way that makes it hard to even realize that it's affecting us the way it is.

We behave in certain ways towards money, simply because these sorts of ideas are so deeply ingrained in us, that we don't even know that's the reason why.

In order to overcome these ideas, you must shift your mindset.

Don't think of money as evil, or as something that's never around, and expect it to be there when you need it.

You will subconsciously get rid of it whenever you have it, because you become fearful of its corruption.

You will waste it, squander it, because you think if you have any extra, something bad might happen that will take it away.

To shift this thinking in myself, even still, I try to be grateful for every dime. This may seem a tad silly, that it is just a superficial fix, but it genuinely works.

Whenever I receive money, I verbally thank God for it. Out loud. Even when people are around.

I write "thank you" on checks, even when it's for paying a bill, simply because I'm grateful that I have the money to pay it.

I check in on my accounts every single morning. This helps me make sure no one is siphoning money, and it keeps me focused on what I can and cannot spend.

I don't love money, but I do love having the ability to pay my bills and help other people when I can; and those are two completely different things.

FOUR

Money Mindset

In addition to the two maxims from the last chapter, a whole lot of us have completely other issues surrounding money.

My paternal grandparents always had a lot of it; my parents did not. My dad, having grown up with it, spent money like they did.

His mantra was basically, "life is short, I'll just pay it off later."

He borrowed a lot of money from my grandma, and though he always paid it back (eventually), it was a constant cycle.

My mom worked at times while I was growing up, with the longest employment stint being probably two years while I was in the 5th and 6th grades.

My dad was a paramedic/firefighter in a very small market, so the salary wasn't great.

We never had a whole lot.

What this created for me was a mindset of scarcity.

For much of my life, I've always believed that money was scarce, and when I had it, I'd better spend it before it ran off on its own.

I STILL believe this sometimes.

*****

Another money mindset issue many, particularly women, have is that they don't feel like they deserve to spend money on themselves.

This mindset rarely shows up for men in the same way as men generally don't take issue buying something that they want.

Women, however, make excuses for why it's too much and will rationalize reasons to not make the purchase. Or if it's in regards to charging for their services when self-employed, they always go low, because they don't think they are worth the higher price tag.

Why is this? Why do so many women have no problem buying things for their children, or other people, but when it's time to spend money on themselves, they balk?

Men are more likely to upgrade to premium when asked. Men are more likely to buy something simply because they want it and will do so without guilt.

Men are entirely more likely to charge more for the work they do simply because they are more likely to have a higher self-worth

*****

Because my dad would always just buy me what I wanted, regardless of whether he had the money to do it or not, I also developed another dangerous mindset about money.

"I don't need to worry about money, somehow things always work themselves out."

This has been true for me my whole life. Somehow, some way, I am always able to get the money I need.

The danger in this is that I have more of a grasshopper mentality than an ant.

Now that I say that, this is the exact difference between the way I think about money, and the way my husband does.

If you aren't familiar with the story, I'll recap quickly.

So, in one of Aesop's Fables, he tells the story of a grasshopper who lives near an ant.

The ant works his tail off (figuratively) all summer, prepping for the winter.

The grasshopper, however, dances. Lives it up.

The ant keeps warning the grasshopper that winter is inevitable. The grasshopper agrees and keeps partying.

In the end, the grasshopper is miserable and starving, and begs the ant for help.

The ant refuses, and the grasshopper dies.

Luckily, my husband (the ant) loves me (the grasshopper), and always bails me out.

In fact, he's always bailed me out. All the way back to when I was living alone and didn't make enough money to actually pay the rent for the apartment I was living in.

So, technically, I'm right, the money IS always there, but if I'm ever going to actually build up my own acumen with money, I've got to stop behaving like the grasshopper.

*****

This next one is nothing but self-righteous baloney.

"God calls us to be humble; spiritual people are not supposed to have money."

No. Just no.

This is the kind of thinking that religious institutions like to keep their parishioners thinking because it helps them maintain control.

It's been going on for centuries.

*****

"Saving $10 a week is never going to get me enough for retirement."

True, sort of.

If you are 45 years old and you are finally starting to save, $10 a week isn't going to cover your retirement, no.

But, it's certainly a place to start, and it might take you somewhere nice.

(Also, if you are 45 and you are just now starting to worry about retirement, we have other stuff we need to discuss, okay?)

Just start a savings account and put money in it regularly. You will be surprised how quickly it all adds up.

*****

A classic one is, "I'm just not destined to have money."

Nope. Not how it works.

*****

And, finally, the big daddy of them all; the one I say,

even now.

"I'm just not good with money."

It is true that I was not raised in a way that taught me how to be good with money.

This does not in any way impact my ability to learn this skill now.

I have a husband that is great with money, and while logic says to just let him handle it, that's not exactly ideal.

What happens to me if something happens to him? I just squander everything he set up for us?

Yeah, the better option is to stop making excuses and learn.

These examples are by no means exhaustive. You may have issues with money that I've never even considered.

Take the space on the next page to write down some negative thoughts you have about money.

On the page after that, write down ways that you can flip a switch and change your thinking.

*How do I feel about money?
How does money make me feel?*

What are some of my negative beliefs regarding money?

How can I flip the switch on this negative mindset?

FIVE

Identify Your Why

A wrong mindset about money isn't the only reason you might spend more than you bring in.

Typically, there are some deep-seated issues. I know I have them. If you want to solve your money problems, you have to take a good hard look at WHY you spend the way you do.

As I said before, my dad would buy almost anything I asked for, whether he had the money or not. But I got to a place where I recognized that he would do that to his own detriment, so I stopped asking.

I knew my parents didn't have the money, and I also knew he wouldn't say no. But I didn't want to be the reason that they were always behind financially.

I often would wait and add things to my Christmas list for my grandparents. Or I'd do chores to earn money to buy those things for myself.

I learned from an early age not to be a burden to other people, and that sometimes you just have to do without.

Fast forward to the early days of being married. As I said previously, things were tight.

Looking back now, I appreciate that I made it through college with no debt. Without my husband's budgeting skills, however, that wouldn't have been possible.

Going from being an independent person who didn't always have the money, but always found a way to get it, to being half of a couple who just blindly turned all her money over to someone else to handle was not something I embraced easily.

I went from a scrappy girl who got what she wanted, to a wife who had to ask for money to buy a new shirt. And that was a hard transition.

On top of all of that, I'm just fiercely independent; it's one of my fatal flaws.

So, there I was with two little kids, a husband who was great, but worked a lot, and was exhausted at the end of every day. I had no hobbies, no outside interests.

I felt like a trapped wolverine.

I needed to do something. Anything. And buying

stuff filled the void.

I bought stuff for my kids. I bought stuff to decorate my house. I bought stuff for my husband. On very rare occasions, I might even actually buy something for myself.

One Christmas, there were so many things for the kids it looked like Santa had just emptied his entire bag of gifts in our living room and told all the other kids in the world to figure it out.

I had started mystery shopping by this point, so I had money coming in, but I wasn't sticking to the amounts allotted for each shop.

I was making money, but it was all going towards debt that my husband didn't know existed.I began paying for cable TV and the groceries, so I was no longer bound by his rules about spending,but I wasn't actually making enough to cover those expenses AND the debt, so I would use credit cards to pay for the difference.

It was a vicious cycle.

When I sat down to analyze exactly WHY I was stuck in this hole, I realized that for me, it was all about not being controlled.

I am not, nor have I ever been a control freak, because I do not want to be controlled.

I rebel against any form of control without even thinking about it.

But how can I change that feeling in regards to money?

Step one was to recognize my issues.

Once I truly understood what was going on in my subconscious, it made it easier to address those issues.

Did I think my husband was actually trying to control me? Or was he just trying to make sound decisions and keep us out of debt?

It was, of course, the latter. He wanted us to end up in our forties with a nice solid financial portfolio, not living paycheck to paycheck, and able to do what we wanted when we wanted.

He was successful with his plan in spite of every wrench I tried to throw in it.

Take a good hard look at your why. If you can figure out what it is, you have a great chance of making actual change in how you handle your money.

SIX

Budget is not a bad word

There is only one thing in this world that I resist stronger than a routine and that's a budget.

But if you are going to get your money stuff under control, a budget is essential.

You absolutely must know where your money is being spent, at all times.

I'd paid my BIG debt off about 9 years ago at this point. I refused to ponder declaring bankruptcy because I knew I would just make the same mistakes again and again.

I firmly believed that the pain of paying off all that money would prevent me from ever making the same mistake repeatedly.

I was wrong.

It's not that I went out and got into a huge amount of debt again. No, I had learned THAT lesson. I never let it get too far out of control to where it was no longer manageable.

But I did keep making the same money mistakes. Over. And over. And over.

I wasn't using a budget.

I wasn't thinking about purchases before I made them.

I wasn't carefully watching where my money was going.

I certainly wasn't saving.

What's more, I paid an arm and a leg in overdraft fees before I realized that I was totally mucking everything up again.

About two years ago, I started really trying. It was hard.

No, it was excruciating.

I hated every single second of looking at my empty bank accounts; scrimping to save every penny and doing without things that I really wanted because I didn't have room in the budget.

It got better though.

I trained myself as if I were training for a marathon: A money marathon. The end goal was more money in the bank and less worry on my mind.

Trust me, it's worth it.

So, how do you train yourself to become a budgeter?

First, you have to recognize that a budget is your friend.

A budget is not to deprive you of the things you want, it instead helps manage your money, so eventually you have enough of it in the bank to buy what you want when you want it.

At the same time, it teaches you to be more careful about what it is you need.

Let's face it, we live in a society where needs vs.wants have a very shady line between them. We can very easily convince ourselves that something we vaguely want is something we actually need to be happy.

After a great deal of trial and error, I've come up with a method to discern how badly I really need any particular item.

Note: This doesn't apply to essentials such as food, electricity, heat, etc.

So, this is how it goes.

I am at a store (or online and see an ad) where

something catches my fancy.

It might be a shirt. Or a swimsuit. Or a new hairband. Or a rug with a giant octopus on it that I really, really, really want for my office.

I note the date I see this item and force myself to wait for two weeks before I can purchase it.

I do NOT write the date down, but just mentally jot it down. The reason for this is if it was written down, I'd remember it for sure.

At the end of two weeks, I've usually forgotten all about whatever it was I thought I wanted so badly. If I haven't, I check to make sure I have the money, and if I do, I will make the purchase.

I still really want that octopus rug, but I've been putting it off for more than two months now. Simply because every time I remember it, I put it off another two weeks.

SEVEN

Step by Step: How I Paid It Off

*I*f you've ended up in the kind of debt I did, I'm betting you've also spent a long time not knowing exactly how much debt you were in.

I took the ostrich approach to it all and just flat out ignored it until every card was maxed, and couldn't be ignored any longer.

I was mystery shopping regularly, but I was to the point that the amount coming in wasn't anywhere near what was needed to make the minimum payments, let alone sustain the other bills I was responsible for.

Something had to give.

If you harken back to page 13, you'll recall that I encouraged you to do an activity.

It was at this point that I realized that I was in a deep mess. Deeper than I ever could have ever imagined.

It was time to get creative.

I attempted to substitute teach for a few months, but the fact of the matter wasI was only making $90 a day with $75 of that going to childcare.

You can see how that might be counterproductive.

Plus, the added stress of dealing with babysitters and anxious kids who just wanted to hang on me all night because they hadn't seen me all day was more than anyone could handle.

My kids were obviously not school age yet, and wouldn't be any time soon, so I had to find something that let me work from home.

I started scouring the Internet for possible work. I found a lot of "get paid to take surveys" and the like, but nothing felt solid.

I started writing for a few websites by watching specific television shows and writing recaps. I got paid $25 per episode.

Clearly, that wasn't going to help make ends meet, but it did give me a lot of good portfolio material, so it wasn't all for naught.

The search continued. Prior to having kids, I'd worked for a Christian television station as a producer of two shows and as an Administrative Assistant to the station manager. So, while perusing Craigslist for jobs (again, this was before people got murdered answering Craigslist ads) I happened upon a fellow looking for a "virtual assistant," and thought, "Hey, I can do that."

I applied to the gig and the fellow agreed to give me a chance. He paid me $8 an hour (promising that once his project started making money he would double everything he ever paid me, but I'm still waiting on that paycheck to arrive).

We worked together for a few months, and while I was doing okay on the debt, paying it down slowly but surely, I was still participating in mystery shopping because it was a money maker, too.

It was not helping though, because I still had the same bad habits of spending more than the allotted amount for each shop.

It hurt, but I had to go cold turkey. No more mystery shopping, no matter what.

I switched to working full-time (and then some) for the Craigslist guy.

That project was forever needing something; a new developer, a new CEO, a new CFO, until eventually

Craigslist guy asked me to post about these positions on a website called HireMyMom.com.

I'd never heard of such a thing, and after posting his jobs, I promptly joined the site myself.

There were tons of legit work from home opportunities, with the side bonus of a host of legitimate clients to choose from.

I had no problem finding a number of new clients.

One was a nutritionist for whom I wrote and designed newsletters.

Another was a life coach who had written a book and was just coming into her real fame. She's a pretty big deal now and we worked together for two solid years. I learned more from her than I could have ever expected and because of her, I met one of the best friends I've ever had.

Eventually, I dropped Craigslist guy because the stress he gave me wasn't worth what he was paying me, and I found better clients who paid more.

We are now about two years into my virtual assistance business, and I'm making enough money to pay my bills and I've paid my debt down to about $52,000.

During this time period, I noticed that I wasn't really doing much to put a dent into that debt. I was doing okay, but not knocking it out as quickly as I'd hoped.

I headed back to the Internet where I found a group called American Consumer Credit Counseling (they are called something different now).

We did a call to analyze my debt, what I owed, and what my interest rates were. They helped me create a budget that was feasible AND that made large payments possible.

This was when I looked at my monthly bills and realized that I was paying for things I wanted, not what I needed, and made some drastic cuts.

I kept our cable TV, but cut it back to the bare minimum. It was nice to have unlimited data on my phone, but it wasn't absolutely necessary, so I dropped my package.

I started watching very carefully what I was buying for groceries, began clipping coupons, and sticking hardcore to the budget that had been designed.

In the meantime, the credit counseling company spoke to all my creditors and got my interest rates lowered in addition to consolidating the payments.

Finally, they called me with a payment plan. Every month I would send them $795. They would distribute my payments to my various credit card accounts, and I paid them a nominal fee in exchange for their service.

I was also able to make extra payments directly to

the card when I could.

At this point, I had no intention of telling my husband about the debt until it was paid off, but the stress of the whole situation was getting to me.

I had a long chat with God about the whole situation and He let me know it was time to come clean with my partner.

I decided to ignore that directive from God for several months. Growing more and more distracted and stressed out as time passed.

The day I finally told my husband, I had paid the debt down to $48,000.

He was angry. Obviously.

I went to his parent's house for the night to give him time to cool off, but when I came back the next day we worked it out.

Well, it wasn't quite that simple, but we found a way to make it work.

I'd borrowed money from him without asking so I could make some of the due dates on my bills (always paying him back), and generally broke his trust to the point that we separated our checking accounts.

He was, overall, very kind about the whole situation. More than could have been expected of anyone, for sure.

I continued to work and raise the kids. He continued his teaching job (I'll tell you more about this in the next chapter).

Every month I made my big payment to the credit counseling group, but I also made side payments to the card with the biggest balance.

This is a technique called the "debt avalanche" and you may have heard of it.

You hit that big card with everything you've got, while making the minimum payment to the rest of the cards.

Before you know it, that whole card is paid off.

My big payment remained the same, but I notified them that the one card was paid off.

They took the extra money and sent it to the card with the highest interest rate and I sent my extra payment to the next biggest card.

It went on like this until I only had one card left. In just a few payments, it was done, too.

And just like that, the debt was paid.

Thanks to the credit counseling company and the extra payments I was making, I paid it off almost exactly two years from the time I made the decision to consolidate the payments.

It wasn't easy. It sucked massively. But even now I don't call it a mistake. I'll explain why in the next chapter.

EIGHT

There Are No Mistakes

So that's it. That's how I did it.

But that's not really the end of the story, is it?

I know that most people would look at my credit card history and say, "Well that was a huge mistake."

But I've never thought of it that way. Not even once.

It was a necessary experience. It caused me to take a good hard look at my life, was what I wanted it to be, and to change things.

If I hadn't gotten into debt, I wouldn't have started my business.

If I hadn't started my business, I wouldn't have met the people I've met. I wouldn't have learned the things I've learned. And I certainly wouldn't have been to half the places I've been.

But perhaps the most important thing is that it got my husband out of a career that he despised and into running his own business, too.

Now we work when we want. We take a Thursday off to get groceries and lunch. Or we go camping for a week (and I still work, because I can work from anywhere, and I LOVE what I do).

It's just like any other big life change that seems both scary and difficult;like getting fired from a dead-end job you've been hating for years, but are just too comfortable to actually do anything about it.

It hurts. It's scary. But it's truly the best thing that could have happened, because it pushes you to make the move that you were resisting.

Sometimes, usually more often than we like, God uses difficult situations to push us to change things that we need changed.

It's so easy for us to become complacent and to just stay put because it's easier and it's familiar.

But nature and the universe do not like stagnation and will do what it takes to adjust the situation.

Stagnation is a sign of a bigger problem, of something deeper that needs to be fixed. If you can't recognize it and take steps to change things, God will change them for you.

So, if you find yourself in a situation similar to the one I found myself in, don't beat yourself up about it.

You may have made some less than stellar choices to get you where you are, but they were divinely designed to put you in this uncomfortable situation and will take you down roads you've never thought about heading down.

It will open doors you never would have pondered knocking on.

It will allow you to climb mountains that previously seemed insurmountable.

Someday you will thank God for the journey. Trust me.

NINE

Bonus Shiz

Alright, so that's it. I can't think of a single other thing to tell you.

But, I do want to give you some tools to help you get rid of your own debt.

Next, you will find a few sample worksheets to show you the kind of records you need to start keeping.

You can head over to MomVsDebt.com/freebies to download a full printable version of the following worksheets (and more bonuses!).

It's time to get your accounts under control. At the pinnacle of my debt, I really didn't even know how many accounts I had open.

Use the worksheet to the right and write down as much info as you are willing. This can serve to help you be aware of how many accounts you have and help you maintain a place where all your log in info is kept. (Be smart, though - and stick this info somewhere safe.)

Account Numbers & Logins

BANK: _____
ACCOUNT: _____
ID NUMBER: _____
ROUTING #: _____
USERNAME: _____
PASSWORD: _____

BANK: _____
ACCOUNT: _____
ID NUMBER: _____
ROUTING #: _____
USERNAME: _____
PASSWORD: _____

BANK: _____
ACCOUNT: _____
ID NUMBER: _____
ROUTING #: _____
USERNAME: _____
PASSWORD: _____

BANK: _____
ACCOUNT: _____
ID NUMBER: _____
ROUTING #: _____
USERNAME: _____
PASSWORD: _____

ACCOUNT: _____
ID NUMBER: _____
ROUTING #: _____
USERNAME: _____
PASSWORD: _____

ACCOUNT: _____
ID NUMBER: _____
ROUTING #: _____
USERNAME: _____
PASSWORD: _____

ACCOUNT: _____
ID NUMBER: _____
ROUTING #: _____
USERNAME: _____
PASSWORD: _____

ACCOUNT: _____
ID NUMBER: _____
ROUTING #: _____
USERNAME: _____
PASSWORD: _____

ACCOUNT: _____
ID NUMBER: _____
ROUTING #: _____
USERNAME: _____
PASSWORD: _____

ACCOUNT: _____
ID NUMBER: _____
ROUTING #: _____
USERNAME: _____
PASSWORD: _____

I included this table earlier in the book, but wanted to put it here with a little more information.

You need to write down every single debt you have. Even if it's $100 you owe your sister. Write it down.

Do not let this procecss scare you. Just get it done. Get a handle on what you owe, so you can make a plan to pay it off.

Actual Debt Analysis

BILL	STARTING BALANCE	INTEREST RATE	MINIMUM PAYMENT	DATE PAID OFF
			$	
			$	
			$	
			$	
			$	
			$	
			$	
			$	
			$	
			$	
			$	
			$	
			$	
			$	
			$	
			$	
			$	
			$	
			$	
			$	
			$	
			$	
			$	
			$	
			$	
			$	
			$	
			$	

TOTAL BILLS AMOUNT $

There are several methods out there for paying off debt. The debt snowball is a popular one. But for me, the only one that made sense is the debt avalanche.

It goes like this:

Make minimum payments on every debt, across the board. On time. Every month.

Pay your other bills.

Take every extra dime you have and pay it on the debt that has the biggest balance. For me, that was also the card with the highest interest rate.

Repeat every month until that one is paid off.

Then move down to the next largest balance.

And do it again.

Before you know it, you are debt free.

Debt Avalanche Plan

START WITH THE MINIMUM PAYMENT ON ALL DEBT
ONCE #1 IS PAID OFF ADD #1'S MINIMUM PAYMENT TO #2
ONCE #2 IS PAID OFF ADD #2'S MINIMUM PAYMENT TO #3
AND SO ON...

	#1	#2	#3	#4
DEBT NAME:				
DEBT BALANCE:	$	$	$	$
DEBT APR %:	%	%	%	%
MIN. PAYMENT:	$	$	$	$
MONTH 1	$	$	$	$
MONTH 2	$	$	$	$
MONTH 3	$	$	$	$
MONTH 4	$	$	$	$
MONTH 5	$	$	$	$
MONTH 6	$	$	$	$
MONTH 7	$	$	$	$
MONTH 8	$	$	$	$
MONTH 9	$	$	$	$
MONTH 10	$	$	$	$
MONTH 11	$	$	$	$
MONTH 12	$	$	$	$
MONTH 14	$	$	$	$
MONTH 15	$	$	$	$
MONTH 16	$	$	$	$
MONTH 17	$	$	$	$
MONTH 18	$	$	$	$
MONTH 19	$	$	$	$
MONTH 20	$	$	$	$
MONTH 21	$	$	$	$
MONTH 22	$	$	$	$
MONTH 23	$	$	$	$
MONTH 24	$	$	$	$
MONTH 25	$	$	$	$
MONTH 26	$	$	$	$
MONTH 27	$	$	$	$
MONTH 28	$	$	$	$
MONTH 29	$	$	$	$
MONTH 30	$	$	$	$
MONTH 31	$	$	$	$
MONTH 32	$	$	$	$
MONTH 33	$	$	$	$
MONTH 34	$	$	$	$
MONTH 35	$	$	$	$
MONTH 36	$	$	$	$

In order to successfully start managing your money, you need to know how much you've got coming in every month. For me, that number is highly variable.

The comfort of a normal job comes with the comfort of know exactly how much to expect every month, and gives you the ability to find ways to supplement that.

If you are running your own business, you have to be a little more careful. Some months are like a farmer's bumper crop. Others are more like the dry season.

Your specific circumstances will dictate how often you need to revisit this.

Monthly Income

MONTH: _____

DATE	SOURCE	AMOUNT
		$
		$
		$
		$
		$
		$
		$
		$
		$
		$
		$
		$
		$
		$
		$
		$
		$
		$
		$
		$
		$
		$
		$
		$
		$
		$
		$
		$
		$
		$

TOTAL MONTHLY EXPENSES $ _____

Now that you know how much should be coming in, you can look at how much is going out.

List every single expense. Lotto tickets too.

This isn't the time to be worried about what other people think of your spending habits, just list them all out. No one will see this but you.

Monthly Expenses

MONTH:

DATE	EXPENSE	COST
		$
		$
		$
		$
		$
		$
		$
		$
		$
		$
		$
		$
		$
		$
		$
		$
		$
		$
		$
		$
		$
		$
		$
		$
		$
		$
		$
		$
		$
		$
		$

TOTAL MONTHLY EXPENSES $

Let's make a budget!

When you know what you've got coming in, and what you need to spend - that's all you need to create a budget.

You can use the one here, or you can use whatever works for you - but use it.

I currently use an online budget program called You Need A Budget.

Clever and to the point, right?

Amanda Arthur Krill | 79

Monthly Budget

MONTH: _____

ACCOUNT: _____
- STARTING BALANCE: $
- ENDING BALANCE: $

ACCOUNT: _____
- STARTING BALANCE: $
- ENDING BALANCE: $

ACCOUNT: _____
- STARTING BALANCE: $
- ENDING BALANCE: $

ACCOUNT: _____
- STARTING BALANCE: $
- ENDING BALANCE: $

MONTHLY INCOME

SOURCE	AMOUNT
	$
	$
	$
	$
	$
	$
	$
	$
	$
	$
TOTAL MONTLY INCOME	$

MONTHLY BILLS

PAID	BILLS	DUE THIS MONTH	BALANCE LEFT
		$	$
		$	$
		$	$
		$	$
		$	$
		$	$
		$	$
		$	$
		$	$
		$	$
	TOTALS:	$	$

MONTHLY EXPENSES

PAID	EXPENSES	AMOUNT	PAID	EXPENSES	AMOUNT
		$			$
		$			$
		$			$
		$			$
		$			$
		$		TOTALS:	$

INCOME TOTAL: _____ + ACCOUNTS ENDING BALANCE TOTAL: _____ − BILLS TOTAL: _____ − EXPENSES TOTAL: _____
= MONTHLY TOTAL ENDING BALANCE: _____

The key to taking care of your debt in a quick manner is staying on top of your money. At. All. Times.

I check my balances daily, but it's helpful to also keep a weekly log - that way you can see patterns over time. This is especially helpful if you are an entrepreneur.

This also gives you a quick overview to help you when you want something, and you've waited the required two week period. Check your balance. If the extra isn't there, you don't get it.

Weekly Accounts Balance

WEEK: _____

DATE: _____

ACCOUNTS	TOTAL
	$
	$
	$
	$
	$

DATE: _____

ACCOUNTS	TOTAL
	$
	$
	$
	$
	$

DATE: _____

ACCOUNTS	TOTAL
	$
	$
	$
	$
	$

DATE: _____

ACCOUNTS	TOTAL
	$
	$
	$
	$
	$

DATE: _____

ACCOUNTS	TOTAL
	$
	$
	$
	$
	$

DATE: _____

ACCOUNTS	TOTAL
	$
	$
	$
	$
	$

DATE: _____

ACCOUNTS	TOTAL
	$
	$
	$
	$
	$

Time flies, even when you are not having fun. Sometimes it feels like you just paid that bill, and it's time to pay it again.

Use this table to keep track of what you paid and when, and you won't ever lose track of how long it's actually been.

Monthly Bill Payment

MONTH: _____

PAID	BILL	DUE DATE	AMOUNT	BALANCE LEFT
○			$	$
○			$	$
○			$	$
○			$	$
○			$	$
○			$	$
○			$	$
○			$	$
○			$	$
○			$	$
○			$	$
○			$	$
○			$	$
○			$	$
○			$	$
○			$	$
○			$	$
○			$	$
○			$	$
○			$	$
○			$	$
○			$	$
○			$	$
○			$	$
○			$	$
○			$	$

MONTHLY REVENUE $ _____
−
TOTAL BILLS AMOUNT $ _____
=
$ LEFT AFTER BILLS $ _____

I know it seems like being in debt and saving at the same time doesn't make a lot of sense. Do it anyway.

Even if you are only saving ten dollars a week, do it.

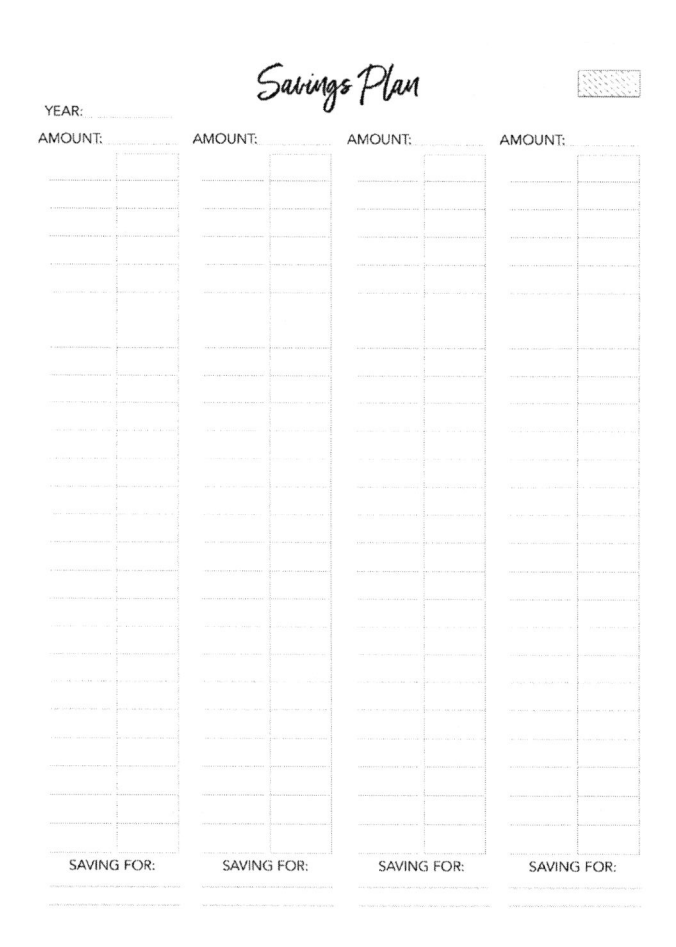

Savings Plan

YEAR:

AMOUNT:	AMOUNT:	AMOUNT:	AMOUNT:

SAVING FOR: SAVING FOR: SAVING FOR: SAVING FOR:

Seriously, look at these sample plans for saving ten, twenty-five or even fifty dollars a week and look at what it gets you!

It won't let you retire - but you could definitely have some fun.

52 Weeks $10 Savings Plan

SAVINGS ACCOUNT: _____
SAVING FOR: _____

DATE	SAVINGS AMOUNT	TOTAL SAVED	SAVED	DATE	SAVINGS AMOUNT	TOTAL SAVED	SAVED
WEEK 1	$10	$10	○	WEEK 27	$10	$270	○
WEEK 2	$10	$20	○	WEEK 28	$10	$280	○
WEEK 3	$10	$30	○	WEEK 29	$10	$290	○
WEEK 4	$10	$40	○	WEEK 30	$10	$300	○
WEEK 5	$10	$50	○	WEEK 31	$10	$310	○
WEEK 6	$10	$60	○	WEEK 32	$10	$320	○
WEEK 7	$10	$70	○	WEEK 33	$10	$330	○
WEEK 8	$10	$80	○	WEEK 34	$10	$340	○
WEEK 9	$10	$90	○	WEEK 35	$10	$350	○
WEEK 10	$10	$100	○	WEEK 36	$10	$360	○
WEEK 11	$10	$110	○	WEEK 37	$10	$370	○
WEEK 12	$10	$120	○	WEEK 38	$10	$380	○
WEEK 13	$10	$130	○	WEEK 39	$10	$390	○
WEEK 14	$10	$140	○	WEEK 40	$10	$400	○
WEEK 15	$10	$150	○	WEEK 41	$10	$410	○
WEEK 16	$10	$160	○	WEEK 42	$10	$420	○
WEEK 17	$10	$170	○	WEEK 43	$10	$430	○
WEEK 18	$10	$180	○	WEEK 44	$10	$440	○
WEEK 19	$10	$190	○	WEEK 45	$10	$450	○
WEEK 20	$10	$200	○	WEEK 46	$10	$460	○
WEEK 21	$10	$210	○	WEEK 47	$10	$470	○
WEEK 22	$10	$220	○	WEEK 48	$10	$480	○
WEEK 23	$10	$230	○	WEEK 49	$10	$490	○
WEEK 24	$10	$240	○	WEEK 50	$10	$500	○
WEEK 25	$10	$250	○	WEEK 51	$10	$510	○
WEEK 26	$10	$260	○	WEEK 52	$10	$520	○

52 Weeks $25 Savings Plan

SAVINGS ACCOUNT: _____
SAVING FOR: _____

DATE	SAVINGS AMOUNT	TOTAL SAVED	SAVED	DATE	SAVINGS AMOUNT	TOTAL SAVED	SAVED
WEEK 1	$25	$25	○	WEEK 27	$25	$675	○
WEEK 2	$25	$50	○	WEEK 28	$25	$700	○
WEEK 3	$25	$75	○	WEEK 29	$25	$725	○
WEEK 4	$25	$100	○	WEEK 30	$25	$750	○
WEEK 5	$25	$125	○	WEEK 31	$25	$775	○
WEEK 6	$25	$150	○	WEEK 32	$25	$800	○
WEEK 7	$25	$175	○	WEEK 33	$25	$825	○
WEEK 8	$25	$200	○	WEEK 34	$25	$850	○
WEEK 9	$25	$225	○	WEEK 35	$25	$875	○
WEEK 10	$25	$250	○	WEEK 36	$25	$900	○
WEEK 11	$25	$275	○	WEEK 37	$25	$925	○
WEEK 12	$25	$300	○	WEEK 38	$25	$950	○
WEEK 13	$25	$325	○	WEEK 39	$25	$975	○
WEEK 14	$25	$350	○	WEEK 40	$25	$1000	○
WEEK 15	$25	$375	○	WEEK 41	$25	$1025	○
WEEK 16	$25	$400	○	WEEK 42	$25	$1050	○
WEEK 17	$25	$425	○	WEEK 43	$25	$1075	○
WEEK 18	$25	$450	○	WEEK 44	$25	$1100	○
WEEK 19	$25	$475	○	WEEK 45	$25	$1125	○
WEEK 20	$25	$500	○	WEEK 46	$25	$1150	○
WEEK 21	$25	$525	○	WEEK 47	$25	$1175	○
WEEK 22	$25	$550	○	WEEK 48	$25	$1200	○
WEEK 23	$25	$575	○	WEEK 49	$25	$1225	○
WEEK 24	$25	$600	○	WEEK 50	$25	$1250	○
WEEK 25	$25	$625	○	WEEK 51	$25	$1275	○
WEEK 26	$25	$650	○	WEEK 52	$25	$1300	○

52 Weeks $50 Savings Plan

SAVINGS ACCOUNT: _____
SAVING FOR: _____

DATE	SAVINGS AMOUNT	TOTAL SAVED	SAVED	DATE	SAVINGS AMOUNT	TOTAL SAVED	SAVED
WEEK 1	$50	$50	○	WEEK 27	$50	$1350	○
WEEK 2	$50	$100	○	WEEK 28	$50	$1400	○
WEEK 3	$50	$150	○	WEEK 29	$50	$1450	○
WEEK 4	$50	$200	○	WEEK 30	$50	$1500	○
WEEK 5	$50	$250	○	WEEK 31	$50	$1550	○
WEEK 6	$50	$300	○	WEEK 32	$50	$1600	○
WEEK 7	$50	$350	○	WEEK 33	$50	$1650	○
WEEK 8	$50	$400	○	WEEK 34	$50	$1700	○
WEEK 9	$50	$450	○	WEEK 35	$50	$1750	○
WEEK 10	$50	$500	○	WEEK 36	$50	$1800	○
WEEK 11	$50	$550	○	WEEK 37	$50	$1850	○
WEEK 12	$50	$600	○	WEEK 38	$50	$1900	○
WEEK 13	$50	$650	○	WEEK 39	$50	$1950	○
WEEK 14	$50	$700	○	WEEK 40	$50	$2000	○
WEEK 15	$50	$750	○	WEEK 41	$50	$2050	○
WEEK 16	$50	$800	○	WEEK 42	$50	$2100	○
WEEK 17	$50	$850	○	WEEK 43	$50	$2150	○
WEEK 18	$50	$900	○	WEEK 44	$50	$2200	○
WEEK 19	$50	$950	○	WEEK 45	$50	$2250	○
WEEK 20	$50	$1000	○	WEEK 46	$50	$2300	○
WEEK 21	$50	$1050	○	WEEK 47	$50	$2350	○
WEEK 22	$50	$1100	○	WEEK 48	$50	$2400	○
WEEK 23	$50	$1150	○	WEEK 49	$50	$2450	○
WEEK 24	$50	$1200	○	WEEK 50	$50	$2500	○
WEEK 25	$50	$1250	○	WEEK 51	$50	$2550	○
WEEK 26	$50	$1300	○	WEEK 52	$50	$2600	○

When you have variable income, automatic bill pay is not a great idea. But if your income is steady, it's a great way to take care of your bills without needing to remember when they need to be take care of.

Use this tracker to stay on top of your payments.

Automatic Bill Payment

YEAR: _____

ACCOUNT	RECIPIENT	PAYMENT AMOUNT	MONTHLY YEARLY	DATE SCHEDULED	MONTHLY PAYMENT CHECK OFF
		$	○ ○		J F M A M J J A S O N D
		$	○ ○		J F M A M J J A S O N D
		$	○ ○		J F M A M J J A S O N D
		$	○ ○		J F M A M J J A S O N D
		$	○ ○		J F M A M J J A S O N D
		$	○ ○		J F M A M J J A S O N D
		$	○ ○		J F M A M J J A S O N D
		$	○ ○		J F M A M J J A S O N D
		$	○ ○		J F M A M J J A S O N D
		$	○ ○		J F M A M J J A S O N D
		$	○ ○		J F M A M J J A S O N D
		$	○ ○		J F M A M J J A S O N D
		$	○ ○		J F M A M J J A S O N D
		$	○ ○		J F M A M J J A S O N D
		$	○ ○		J F M A M J J A S O N D

Christmas, birthdays, graduations all have to be taken care of, even when you are on a budget. Use this sheet to keep track of what's coming and make it part of the plan.

Holiday/Event/Gift Budget

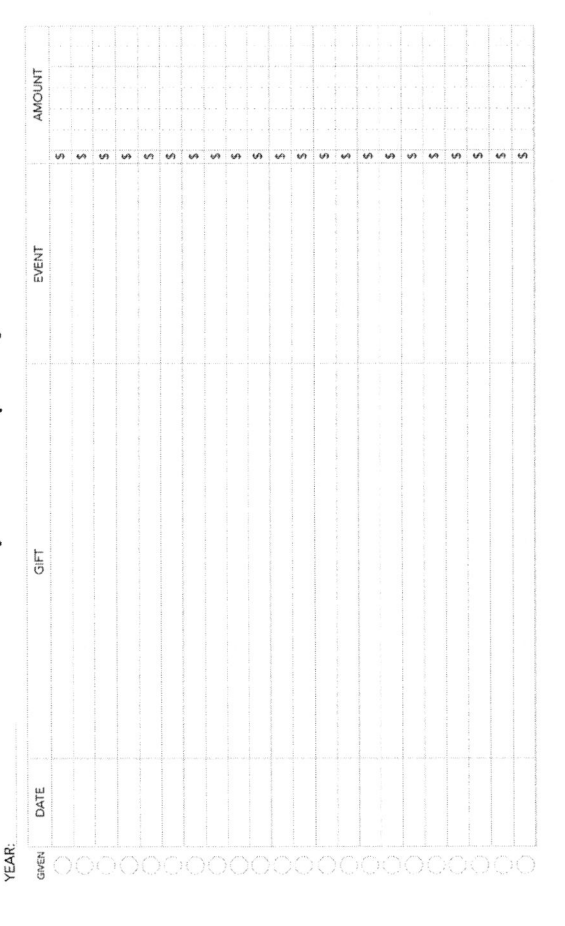

YEAR: _____

GIVEN	DATE	GIFT	EVENT	AMOUNT
○				$
○				$
○				$
○				$
○				$
○				$
○				$
○				$
○				$
○				$
○				$
○				$
○				$
○				$
○				$
○				$
○				$
○				$
○				$
○				$

Acknowledgments

To God be the glory.

Husband & Kids – thank you for tolerating my whims and my gunslinger mentality.

Frances & Paul, Phyllis & Glen, Chick & Pap – without the lot of you, I am sure that I would not be the person I am. Thank you for being the greatest grandparents in the whole world.

Mom & Dad, Aunts & Uncles - you have no idea the impact that you had on me.

Lisa, who is always super honest about all my crazy ideas, and is right there with me for all of them.

And you.

I love you all.

About the Author

Amanda Arthur Krill is a wife and mom to three freaking amazing kids.

She loves Jesus, fish tacos, the Chicago Bears, and the Pittsburgh Pirates.

She was born a Michigander, but raised in Ohio, and spent a month every year in Missouri, so you can imagine that she has some deep-seated issues

Website: www.amandakrill.com | www.justboldlygo.com

Instagram: @amandakrill

Facebook: @amandakrillinc | @justboldlygo

Twitter: @amandakrill

YGT MAMA
MEDIA CO.

Helping Mama's birth their Brain Babies

At YGTMama Media Co. we help mamas bring their visions to life. Through a collaborative and supportive community we truly value the idea that it takes a village as we bring your Brain Baby into this world. We are a unique and boutique publisher and professional branding company that caters to all stages of business around your book and personal brand as an author. We work with seasoned and emerging authors on solo and collaborative projects.

Our mamas have a safe space to grow and diversify themselves within the genres of non-fiction, personal development, spiritual enlightenment, health and wellness, love and relationships, motherhood and business as well as children's books, journals and personal and professional growth tools. We help motivated mamas realize dreams and ideas by breathing life into their powerful passions. We believe in women's empowerment, community over competition and equal opportunity. You are so much more then "just a mom" you've got this, Mama!

Join or connect with The Mama Tribe

Website: www.ygtmama.com | www.ygtmamamedia.co

Instagram: @ygtmama | @ygtmama.media.co

Facebook: @ygtmama | @ygtmama.media.co